FRETBOARD FORENSICS SERIES ™

THE LITTLE GUITAR BOOK THAT COULD

NINTH POSITION

by

Walter Klosowski III

is published exclusively through:

OMNI MUSIC PRESS ®
7308 E 68th Pl Tulsa, OK 74133

http://www.omnimusicpress.com

Written, designed, edited, compiled, printed & distributed by the author.

Order Number OMP 003-009

ISBN 978-0692185605   Library of Congress Control Number: 2020919875

The Little Guitar Book That Could

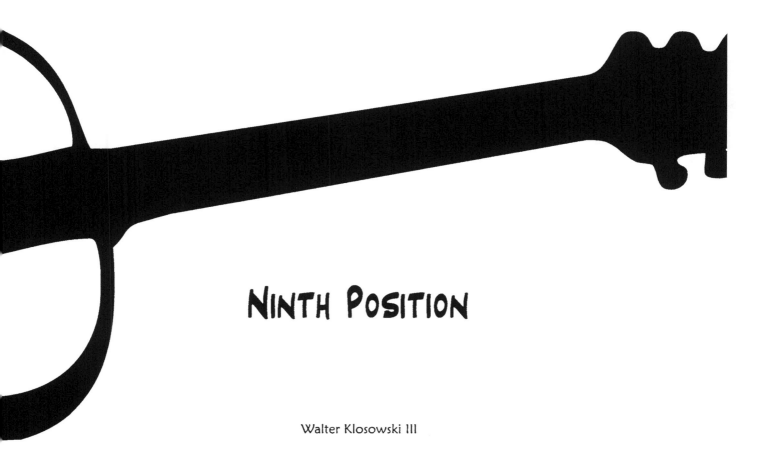

NINTH POSITION

Walter Klosowski III

OMP®

OMNI MUSIC PRESS

This book is dedicated to that astute music theorist found deep within every guitar player, or the lack thereof. As for writing it, I owe a deep personal thank you to my family who supported me and gave of their time during this project. I would also like to thank my guitar/music professors, colleagues, students and friends over the years for candidly answering my questions while sharing their unique opinions and insights.

THE LITTLE GUITAR BOOK THAT COULD...

... SHOWCASES THE C A G E D GUITAR CHORD AND SCALE SEQUENCE EXCLUSIVELY IN THE NINTH POSITION, FOR ALL TO SEE, USE AND REFERENCE. THIS *LITTLE GUITAR BOOK THAT COULD* DOES PRESUME THE FOLLOWING:

1) <u>GUITAR POSITION DETAIL</u> –

ON THE FRETBOARD THERE IS AN OVERT SIX CONSECUTIVE FRET AREA THAT DELINEATES THE NINTH POSITION, AND IT SPANS TWO OCTAVES PLUS A PERFECT FOURTH...

2) <u>FRETTING HAND DETAIL</u> –

THE SECOND AND OR THIRD FINGERS ON THE HAND REMAIN AT THE CORE, IN THEIR CENTERED FRETS. IT'S THE FIRST AND FOURTH FINGERS THAT STRETCH...

3) <u>PICKING HAND DETAIL</u> –

AN IMPORTANT "$(①D^2 -③E^{1-4} -⑤G^2 -②A^2 -④C^2 -⑥D^2)$" PICKING PATTERN OCCURS AS THE C A G E D ROOT NOTE SEQUENCE IS PLUCKED ALPHABETICALLY...

4) MAIN ROOT NOTE DETAIL —

AS A RULE, WHEN IN A GUITAR POSITION, THE **MAIN** ROOT NOTES ARE THOSE FOUND UNDER THE SECOND AND THIRD FINGERS. HOWEVER, THE E **MAIN** ROOT NOTE(S) HERE IN THE NINTH POSITION INVOLVE THE FIRST AND OR FOURTH FINGER(S), MAKING IT AN EXCEPTION OF SORTS...

5) OCTAVE DETAIL —

THE INTERVAL BETWEEN ONE MUSICAL PITCH AND ANOTHER WITH HALF OR DOUBLE ITS OWN FREQUENCY IS KNOWN AS A PERFECT OCTAVE. IN GUITARLAND, THEY ARE TYPICALLY "ONE STRING ONE FRET AWAY". HOWEVER, OCCASIONALLY, TWO STRINGS AND OR TWO FRETS ARE INVOLVED...

6) UNISON DETAIL —

WHEN TWO OR MORE NOTES SOUND THE SAME PITCH IT IS SAID THEY ARE IN UNISON. IN GUITARLAND, IT GENERALLY MEANS "SAME NOTE DIFFERENT STRING OR FRET". AND IT IS ALSO IMPLIED THAT THE UNISON OCCURS IN THE GUITAR POSITION AT HAND...

7) ④TH, 2ND –

SHORTHAND FOR THE ④TH STRING, 2ND FINGER **MAIN** C ROOT NOTE OR "DOT"; ANCHORING THE C MATERIAL...

8) ②ND, 2ND –

SHORTHAND FOR THE ②ND STRING, 2ND FINGER **MAIN** A ROOT NOTE OR "DOT"; ANCHORING THE A MATERIAL...

9) ⑤TH, 2ND –

SHORTHAND FOR THE ⑤TH STRING, 2ND FINGER **MAIN** G ROOT NOTE OR "DOT"; ANCHORING THE G MATERIAL...

10) ①ST ③RD ⑥TH, 1ST & 4TH –

SHORTHAND FOR THE ①ST ③RD ⑥TH STRING(S), 1ST & 4TH FINGER(S) **MAIN** E ROOT NOTE(S) OR "DOT(S)"...

11) ①ST ⑥TH, 2ND –

SHORTHAND FOR THE ①ST ⑥TH STRING(S), 2ND FINGER **MAIN** D ROOT NOTE(S) OR "DOT(S)"; ANCHORING D...

TABLE OF CONTENTS

TABLE OF CONTENTS ...

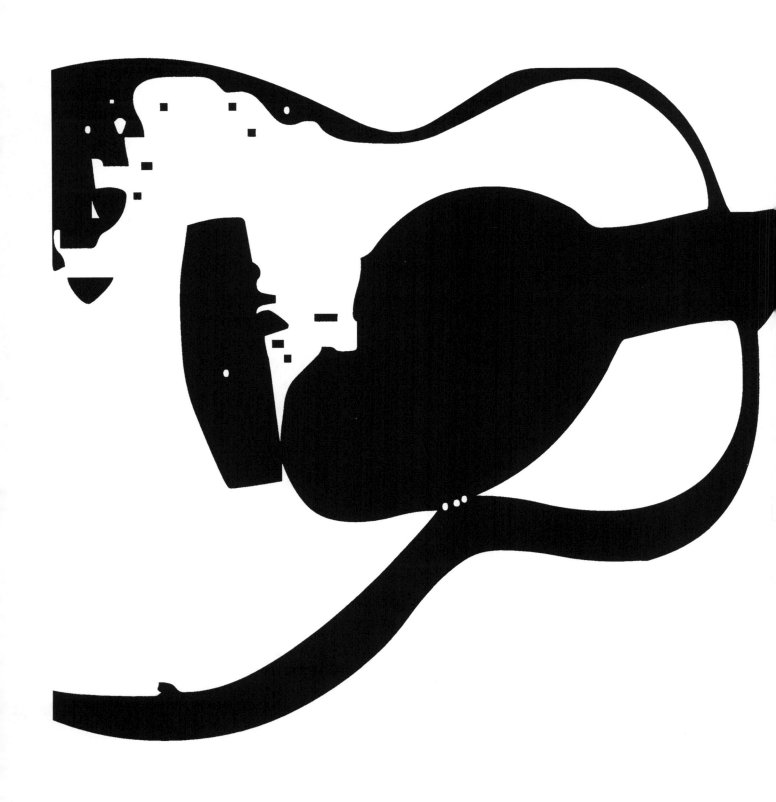

Ninth Position Preface

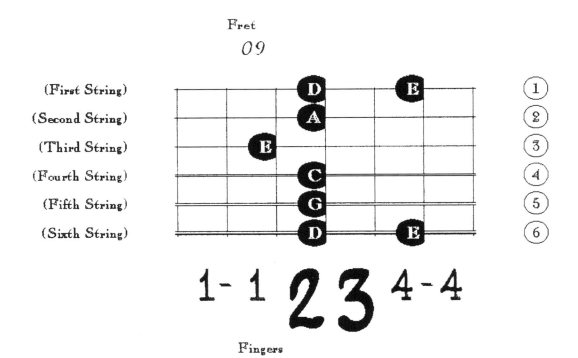

(First String)

(Second String)

(Third String)

(Fourth String)

(Fifth String)

(Sixth String)

1- 1 **2 3** 4 - 4

Fingers

THIS GRID REPRESENTS THE GUITAR'S NINTH POSITION AS FOUND IN THIS BOOK. THE THINNEST STRING IS ON TOP, AND IT HAS SIX CONSECUTIVE FRETS. THE FOUR FINGERS ON THE FRETTING HAND CENTER THEMSELVES INSIDE THE SIX, ONE FINGER PER FRET, LEAVING ONE EMPTY FRET ON EITHER SIDE. THAT SAID, THE SECOND AND THIRD FINGERS REMAIN FIXED IN THE HEART OF THE POSITION, THIS IN TURN ALLOWING THE FIRST AND FOURTH FINGERS ON THE HAND TO STRETCH, OR SLIDE, TO THEIR NOTES LOCATED IN THE OUTERMOST FRET AREAS. THE CENTERED ROOT NOTES BENEATH THE SECOND AND THIRD FINGERS ARE CALLED **MAIN** ROOT NOTES OR, EN MASSE, THE **MAIN** ROOT NOTE CLUSTER.

THEY'RE TYPICALLY FRETTED USING THE SECOND AND THIRD FINGERS, THOUGH HERE THE THIRD FINGER IS NOT REQUIRED. MOREOVER EXCEPTIONS DO EXIST IN THIS POSITION, AS THE E **MAIN** ROOT NOTE(S) OBLIGATE THE FIRST AND OR FOURTH FINGER(S) AS WELL. AN ABRIDGMENT OF THE FINGERING IS DETAILED BELOW.

NINTH GUITAR POSITION, FINGERING DETAIL, COMPLETE WITH STRETCHES

9TH FRET

1-1 2 3 4 -4

⌒ POSITION NUMBER BEHIND SECOND FINGER, ONE FINGER PER FRET [1]

BASICALLY, SINCE THE FIRST FINGER ON THE HAND HAS THE OPPORTUNITY TO STRETCH, THE ATTENTION THEN SHIFTS TO THE EXACT IDENTIFYING NUMBER OF THAT FRET BEHIND THE SECOND FINGER, AS THAT IDENTIFYING NUMBER DETERMINES POSITION LOCALE. GENERALLY SPEAKING, BOTH THE SECOND AND THIRD FINGERS REMAIN FIXED IN THEIR CORE FRETS AS THEY DO NOT STRETCH, AT LEAST FOR NOW. IN TIME, THE FIRST AND FOURTH FINGER FRET AREAS COMBINE WITH THAT CENTERED, THIS DEFINING THE SIX CONSECUTIVE FRET AREA PREVIOUSLY DISCUSSED. LAST, THE NINTH POSITION SPANS JUST TWO OCTAVES, PLUS A PERFECT FOURTH, SO LONG AS THE GUITAR REMAINS IN STANDARD TUNING.

[1] MICK GOODRICK. *THE ADVANCING GUITARIST. APPLYING GUITAR CONCEPTS & TECHNIQUES.* MILWAUKEE, WI. HAL LEONARD MUSIC PUBLISHING. 1987. PAGES 27-29

v

THESE ARE THE FOUR CHORD TYPES PRESENTED IN THIS
BOOK. THE ROWS PROVIDE ALTERNATE VOICING CHOICE.

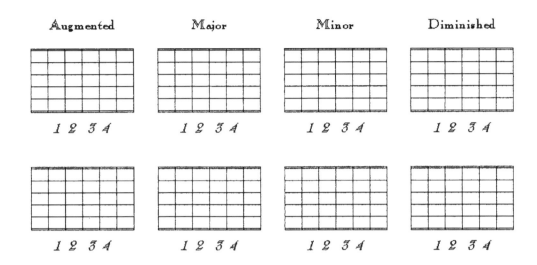

DO UNDERSTAND THAT THE CHORD SEQUENCE PRESENTED IS
DELIBERATE SUCH THAT AS THE EYES TRAVERSE THE IMAGES
FROM LEFT TO RIGHT, OR VISE VERSA, ONLY ONE NOTE WILL
BE ALTERED OR CHANGED. OBSERVE THE AUGMENTED CHORD
BEGINS AS IT MORPHS OVER TO MAJOR, THE FIFTH IN FLUX.
AS THE MAJOR CHORD FOLLOWS, IT THEN MORPHS TO MINOR
WITH THE ALTERED THIRD. IT ENDS WITH THE MINOR CHORD
MORPHING OVER TO THE DIMINISHED VIA THE ALTERED FIFTH.
PLACING THE CHORD MATERIAL IN THIS LIGHT LEAVES LITTLE
TO CHANCE ENHANCING ITS MEMORIZATION. THE GRIDS ATOP
THE PAGE DETAIL THE CHORD TYPE; ANY RELATED MATERIAL,
LIKE THE DOMINANT SEVENTH, IS PLACED BENEATH.

Augmented chord — (brings musical tension)

This chord type consists of one major third interval with yet another major third interval placed on top. From the root, it's a major third with an augmented fifth. The dominant seventh brings tension as well.

Major chord — (brings musical stability)

This chord type consists of one major third interval with one minor third interval stacked on top. From the root, it's a major third interval; but now with a perfect fifth.

Minor chord — (brings musical stability)

This chord type consists of one minor third interval with one major third interval stacked on top. From the root, it's a minor third interval with the familiar perfect fifth as is.

Diminished chord — (brings musical tension)

This unavoidable chord type consists of a minor third interval with another minor third interval stacked on top. Given, it's a minor third with a diminished fifth.

These are the four scale types presented in this book. The rows provide alternate voicing choice.

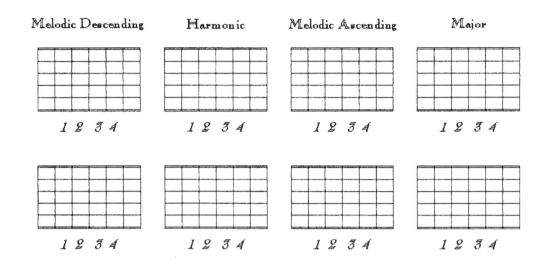

When the eyes traverse the scales left to right, or otherwise, only one note will be altered or changed. Look to see; as the melodic minor descending morphs to the harmonic, only the seventh scale degree will change. From there, as the harmonic minor morphs to the melodic minor ascending (or jazz minor) only the sixth scale degree will change. Last, as the melodic minor ascending morphs to the major scale, only the third scale degree will change. Deliberately putting the material in this light simplifies its learning. The grid row atop details the scale; any related material such as the minor pentatonic is placed beneath.

MELODIC MINOR SCALE DESCENDING FORM

THIS SCALE VARIETY IS IDENTICAL TO THE AEOLIAN, NATURAL OR PURE MINOR. THE MINOR PENTATONIC SCALE IS LIKEWISE DERIVED FROM IT. THE VERY USEFUL "THREE ON A STRING" MINOR PENTATONIC IS PLACED BENEATH THE MELODIC MINOR.

HARMONIC MINOR SCALE

THIS SCALE TYPE IS THE TRADITIONAL MINOR SCALE TAUGHT IN THE VARIOUS MUSIC TEXTBOOKS, SCHOLARLY REFERENCES AND METHODS. IT IS USUALLY PRESENTED AS OPPOSITE TO THAT OF THE MORE BLISSFUL SOUNDING MAJOR SCALE.

MELODIC MINOR SCALE ASCENDING FORM

THIS SCALE TYPE IS ALSO RECOGNIZED AS THE JAZZ MINOR SCALE. IT IS TYPICALLY PRESENTED AS CORRESPONDING TO THE DESCENDING MELODIC MINOR PREVIOUSLY DISCUSSED.

MAJOR SCALE

THIS SCALE TYPE IS MOST SIGNIFICANT. ALL OF THE MAJOR KEYS, ALL OF THE MINOR KEYS, AND ALL OF THE MODES ARE BASED ON IT. IT'S ROUTINELY USED WHEN DEMONSTRATING AND OR CONVEYING OTHER MUSICAL CRITERIA AS WELL.

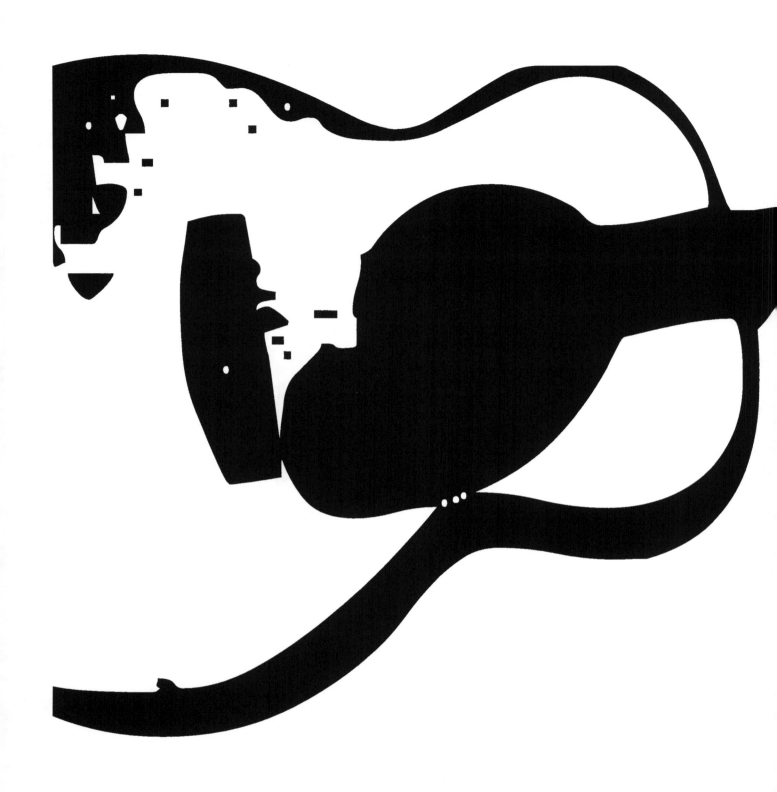

NINTH POSITION

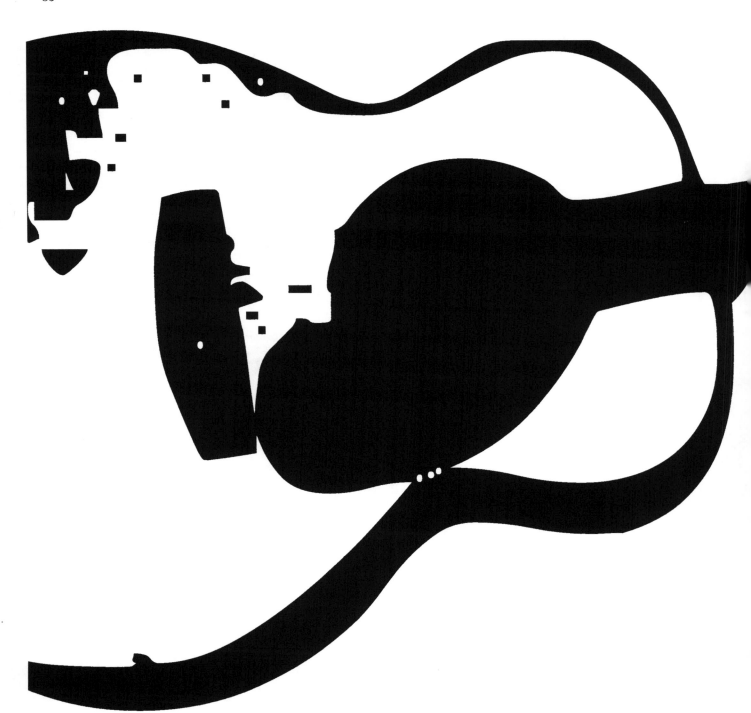

The C Chords and Scales

or
"The ④ᵀᴴ String, 2ᴺᴰ Finger Shapes"

Fret

09

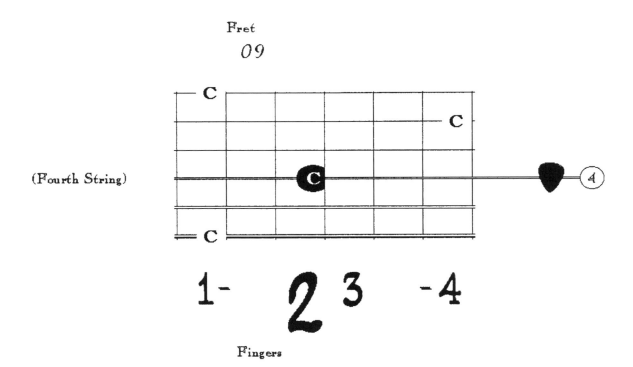

(Fourth String)

1- **2** 3 -4

Fingers

THE NOTABLE "FOURTH STRING SECOND FINGER" SHAPE CONSTRUCT UNDERSCORES ALL THE C CHORDS AND SCALES IN THIS UPPER POSITION. THE **MAIN** C ROOT NOTE IS SITUATED ON THE FOURTH STRING UNDER THE SECOND OR MIDDLE FINGER, THAT FINGER FRETTING. THE LARGE "DOT" GROUNDS THE C FINGER WORK ENTAILED. THE OTHER C'S LOCATED ON THE FIRST AND OR SIXTH STRINGS REQUIRE AN INDEX FINGER STRETCH. SIMILARLY, THE C ON THE SECOND STRING REQUIRES A PINKY STRETCH. ☞

SOME OF THE C CHORD VOICINGS ASSOCIATED WITH THE GUITAR'S NINTH POSITION ARE:

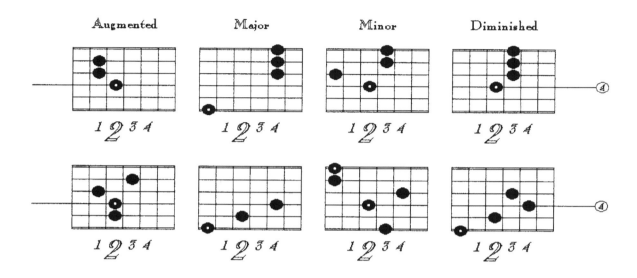

SOME OF THE C SCALE VOICINGS ASSOCIATED WITH THE GUITAR'S NINTH POSITION ARE:

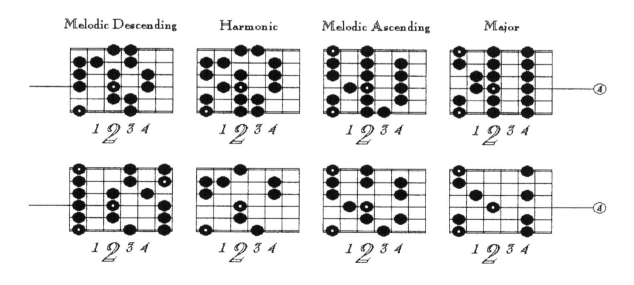

FURTHER COMMENTARY...

IT'S LIKE A PUZZLE SOLVED HOW THE NINTH POSITION C CHORDS AND SCALES FIT TOGETHER SO ASTUTELY. AND KNOW THAT ALL ENSUING FORMS AND PATTERNS LIFTED FROM THIS POSITION WILL PROVE USEFUL IN A VARIETY OF OTHER POSITIONS TOO. THAT SAID, IT IS IMPORTANT TO REALIZE THE TECHNICAL ASPECTS THAT THE SECOND FINGER BRINGS TO THE FINGERING. FOR EXAMPLE, WHEN PLAYING C CHORDS, IT COORDINATES WITH THE PINKY FINGER OFTEN WHEN FRETTING TWO OR MORE STRINGS, PLUS IT SHARES THE SAME SPACE WITH OTHER FINGERS AS IT, THE SECOND OR MIDDLE FINGER, REMAINS THE ANCHOR POINT WHEN FINGERING ISSUES ARISE. THIS HAPPENSTANCE OCCURS BECAUSE THE **MAIN** C ROOT NOTE FALLS UNDER IT. REGARDING THE INDEX FINGER, WITH THE FACT THAT THE C'S ON THE FIRST AND OR SIXTH STRINGS ARE ONE STRETCH

AWAY, THE INDEX FINGER WILL, INADVERTENTLY, END UP FRETTING OR BARRING VARIOUS OTHER STRINGS AT SOME POINT. ALSO, REALIZE THIS FIRST STRING C IS IN UNISON WITH THE SECOND STRING C, THE LATTER NECESSITATING A DISCOMFITED PINKY STRETCH. BUT FOR PRACTICALITY GUITARISTS WILL SOMETIMES SLIDE THE PINKY TO AND FROM IT. LAST AS A FINAL POINT, DON'T FORGET TO INCLUDE THE OPEN STRINGS WHEN PLAYING THIS MATERIAL. OPEN STRINGS IMPROVE THE SONOROUS QUALITIES OF THE VOICINGS, AND INCREASE THE AVAILABLE FINGERING OPTIONS.

ALL C'S DISCLOSED IN THIS SEGMENT ARE MUSICALLY EQUAL. BUT THERE'S NO NEED TO FRET ALL OF THEM ALL THE TIME IN THE C CHORDS AND SCALES PLAYED.

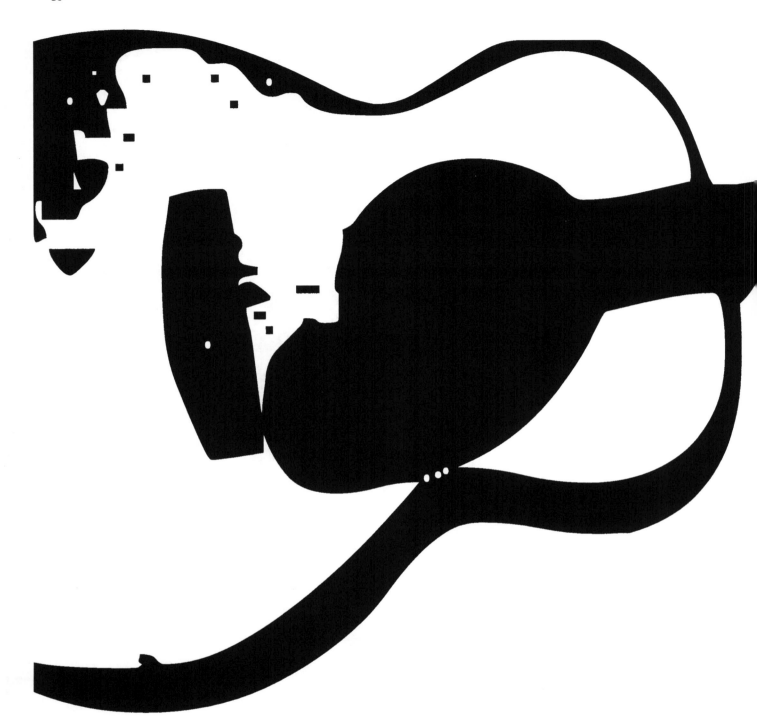

THE A CHORDS AND SCALES

OR

"THE ②ND STRING, 2ND FINGER SHAPES"

Fret
09

(Second String)

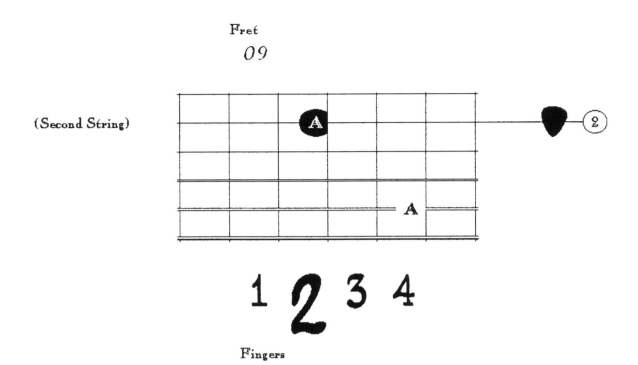

1 **2** 3 4

Fingers

THIS MODISH "SECOND STRING, SECOND FINGER" SHAPE CONSTRUCT UNDERSCORES ALL THE A CHORDS AND SCALES IN THE NINTH POSITION. THE **MAIN** A ROOT NOTE IS LOCATED ON THE SECOND STRING, UNDERNEATH THE SECOND FINGER, AND THE SECOND FINGER FRETS IT. THE "DOT" GROUNDS THE FINGER WORK INVOLVED. NOTICE, THE LOWER OCTAVE A ON THE FIFTH STRING IS FRETTED WITH THE PINKY AND THERE'S NO STRETCHING OF SAID FINGERS WHEN VOICING MATERIAL INSIDE THE SOLITARY OCTAVE. ☞

SOME OF THE A CHORD VOICINGS ASSOCIATED WITH THE GUITAR'S NINTH POSITION ARE:

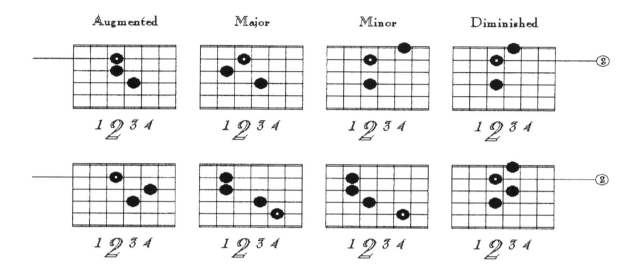

SOME OF THE A SCALE VOICINGS ASSOCIATED WITH THE GUITAR'S NINTH POSITION ARE:

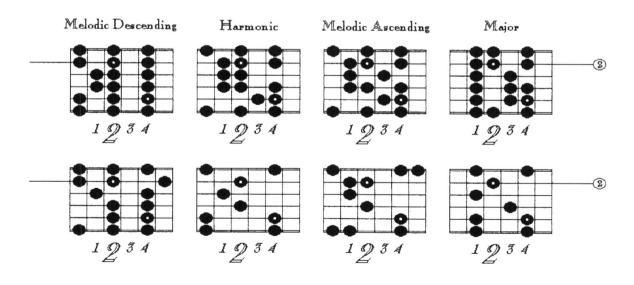

Further Commentary...

The A chords and scales nestle in the confines of the musical framework like creatures do in a tide pool. And any ensuing forms and patterns can be lifted from here and copied in the other positions as well, with slight fingering amends. Here it is taken for granted somewhat how the A chords utilize all six guitar strings in their ordinary expected combinations. However, it is equally important to observe, and it is subtle, that the A scales are predisposed to just the inside set of strings, no thick or thin E, when voiced due to the presence of the only octave. Do recognize this, and compensate accordingly. Both A chord and scale alike though do benefit from open string use, the open fifth A being a prime example of such.

That said, notice the low pitched A on the fifth string, not the previously mentioned open fifth A string, is usually paired with the **MAIN** A root note as seen in the grids. The fourth or pinky finger frets it. This straightforward fingering is much less arduous on the fretting hand, as no other A is available and no finger stretches are involved.

All the A's discussed are considered musically equivalent, identical in purpose and one in the same. But, there's no real need to voice them all the time or all at the same time, regularly or otherwise, in the chords and scales played.

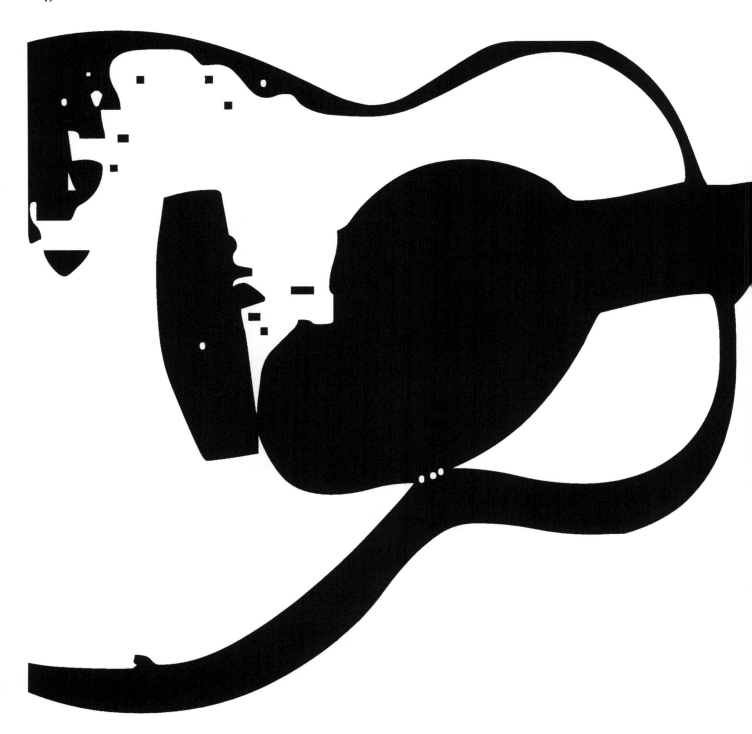

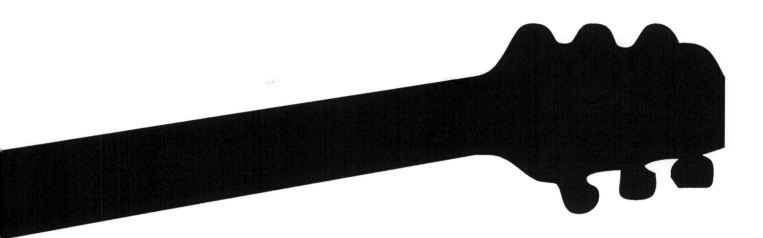

THE G CHORDS AND SCALES

OR
"THE ⑤TH STRING, 2ND FINGER SHAPES"

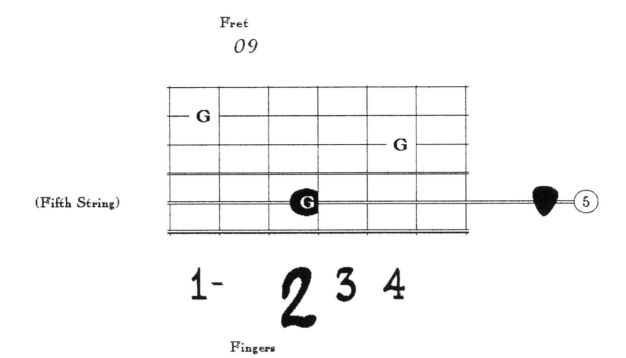

Fret
09

(Fifth String)

1- **2** 3 4

Fingers

T HE CHIC "FIFTH STRING SECOND FINGER" SHAPE CONSTRUCT UNDERSCORES ALL THE G CHORDS AND SCALES IN THE NINTH POSITION. THE ALL IMPORTANT **MAIN** G ROOT NOTE IS CLEARLY FOUND ON THE FIFTH STRING BENEATH THE SECOND FINGER, THE SECOND FINGER FRETTING. CONCERNING THE PAIR OF G'S THAT REMAIN, BOTH ARE HIGHER IN PITCH AND IN UNISON. THE PINKY FINGER FRETS ITS THIRD STRING G EASILY, BUT THE INDEX FINGER MUST STRETCH OR SLIDE TO FRET ITS OWN ON THE SECOND. ☞

SOME OF THE G CHORD VOICINGS ASSOCIATED WITH THE GUITAR'S NINTH POSITION ARE:

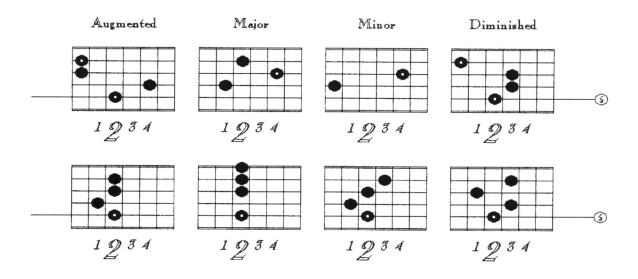

SOME OF THE G SCALE VOICINGS ASSOCIATED WITH THE GUITAR'S NINTH POSITION ARE:

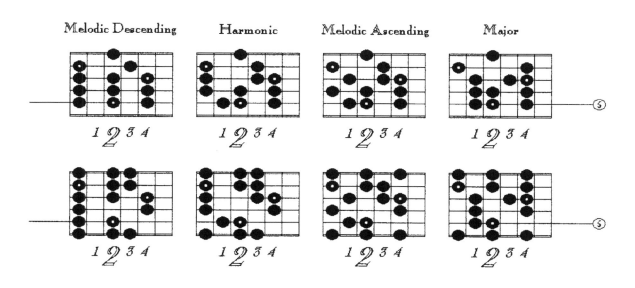

FURTHER COMMENTARY...

ALL G CHORDS AND SCALES MESH WELL TOGETHER IN THE NINTH POSITION, AND THE FOLLOWING FORMS AND PATTERNS FROM HERE WORK JUST FINE IN ANY OTHER POSITION TOO. WHEN PLAYING THESE G CHORDS AND SCALES HERE THOUGH, TECHNICALLY SPEAKING, THERE IS A COORDINATION AMONG THE SECOND AND FOURTH FINGERS, AS THE FIFTH STRING SECOND FINGER "DOT" GROUNDS THE HAND'S WORK. FURTHERMORE, AN OPEN THIRD G STRING AND OR OPEN SECOND B ARE OFTEN INCLUDED IN THIS G MATERIAL, AS THOSE PARTICULAR STRINGS FOSTER THE MORE LAVISH SONORITY. THAT SAID, THE G'S AN OCTAVE AWAY ARE IN UNISON, AND HAVING THE OPEN G AND OR OPEN B JUXTAPOSED AS IT IS AGAINST THIS UNISON PAIR MAKES FOR AN IDEAL MUSICAL HAPPENSTANCE, THIS OFTEN EXPLOITED WITH HARMONICS. TO CONCLUDE, OBSERVE THE G ON THE

THIRD STRING IS TYPICALLY PAIRED WITH THE **MAIN** G ROOT NOTE, AS SEEN IN THE GRIDS, WITH THE PINKY FRETTING FOR OBVIOUS REASONS. BY CONTRAST, THE SECOND STRING G REQUIRES THAT THE INDEX FINGER STRETCH, BUT GUITARISTS CAN SLIDE THE FINGER AS WELL, IF FOR MUSICAL REASONS.

ALL THE G'S DISCUSSED ARE CONSIDERED MUSICALLY EQUAL REGARDING PURPOSE AND FUNCTION. HOWEVER THERE'S NO NEED TO VOICE THEM EVERY TIME OR ALL OF THEM SIMULTANEOUSLY IN THE CHOSEN G CHORDS AND SCALES PLAYED.

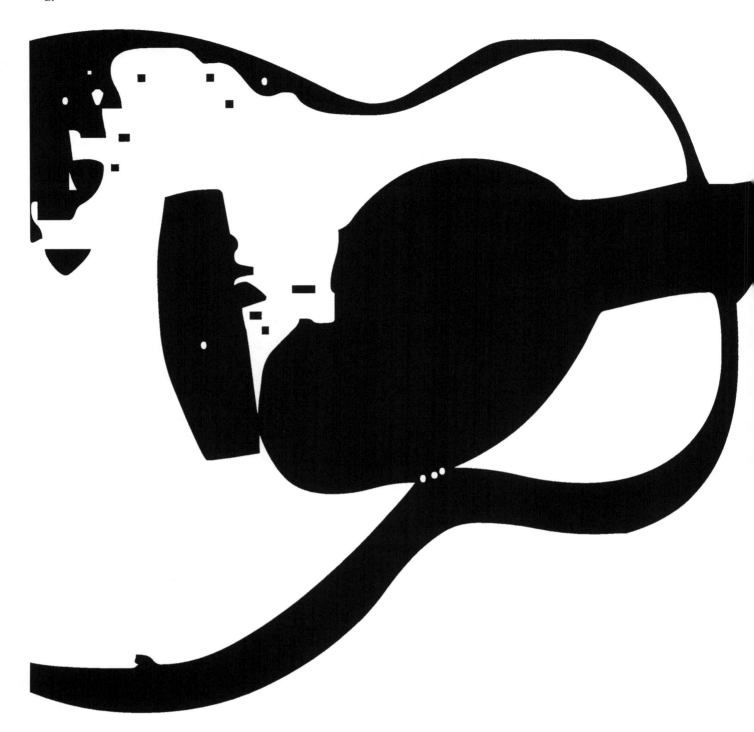

THE E CHORDS AND SCALES

OR
"THE ①st / ③rd / ⑥th STRING(S), 1st & 4th FINGER(S) SHAPES"

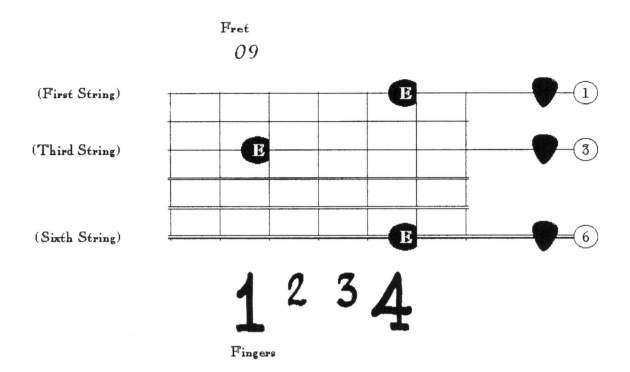

Fret
09

(First String)

(Third String)

(Sixth String)

1 2 3 4
Fingers

THIS SHAPE CONSTRUCT UNDERSCORES EACH E CHORD AND SCALE FOUND HERE IN THE NINTH POSITION, INCLUDING THE COOL E POWER FIVE. OBSERVE, THE FIRST AND OR FOURTH FINGER(S), NOT THE CHARACTERISTIC SECOND AND THIRD, FRET THE E **MAIN** ROOT NOTE(S). THE TRIO OF "DOT(S)" LOCATED ON THE FIRST / THIRD / SIXTH STRING(S) ABET THE FINGERING, HOWEVER FOR CLARITY, NOT ALL E'S NEED TO BE VOICED ALL AT ONCE; THEY DO PAIR OFF QUITE NICELY WHEN PLAYING CHORDS. ☞

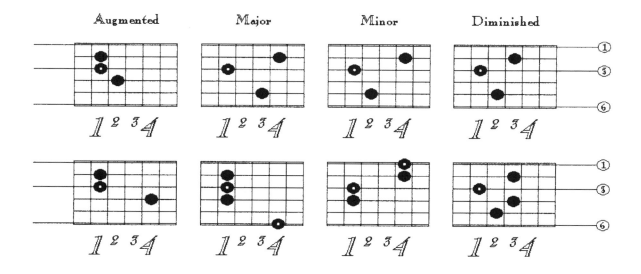
24

SOME OF THE E CHORD VOICINGS ASSOCIATED WITH THE GUITAR'S NINTH POSITION ARE:

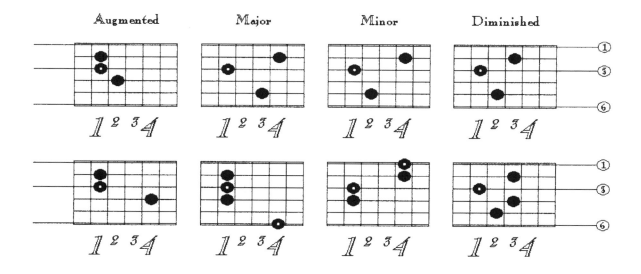

SOME OF THE E SCALE VOICINGS ASSOCIATED WITH THE GUITAR'S NINTH POSITION ARE:

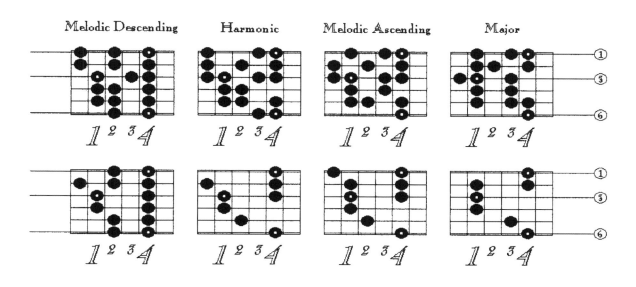

Further Commentary...

All the E chords and scales fit in this position like puzzle pieces do and each subsequent form and pattern from here works perfectly well in any other position too. Also surmise guitarists will often exploit either open E string at will, or even both simultaneously, when voicing this E material, the position here being no exception. The "dot(s)" ground the E finger work involved and bring a fresh sense of feel to the hand, as the construct utilizes the first and or fourth finger(s) in lieu of the second and third. Such coordination results in voicings that are easier to play and understand. Moreover the first or index finger behaves very much like a capo as it navigates these chords and scales, it barring a good deal of the time obviously.

THE FOURTH FINGER ZEALOUSLY FRETS THE THINNEST TOP TWO STRINGS WHEN PLAYING THE DOUBLE STOP, AND THE SAME GOES FOR THE E POWER FIVE, AS THE FOURTH FINGER HOVERS OVER THE NECESSARY NOTES. ALSO, THE PICKING HAND ISSUES CONCERNING STRING SKIPPING ARE BEST UNDERSTOOD IN THIS CONSTRUCT AS THE E'S ARE ALL **MAIN** ROOT NOTE(S), THE LOWER, MIDDLE AND THE UPPER. AND LAST, AS A TECHNICAL BONUS, THERE ARE NO FINGER STRETCHES TO BE HAD WHEN PLAYING THE HIGH OCTAVE.

ALL THREE E'S DISCLOSED IN THIS SEGMENT ARE THE SAME REGARDING THEIR MUSICAL FUNCTION. BUT ALL THREE DON'T NEED TO BE VOICED EVERY TIME OR ALL THE TIME, NOR AT EVERY OPPORTUNITY, IN THE GIVEN E CHORDS AND SCALES PLAYED.

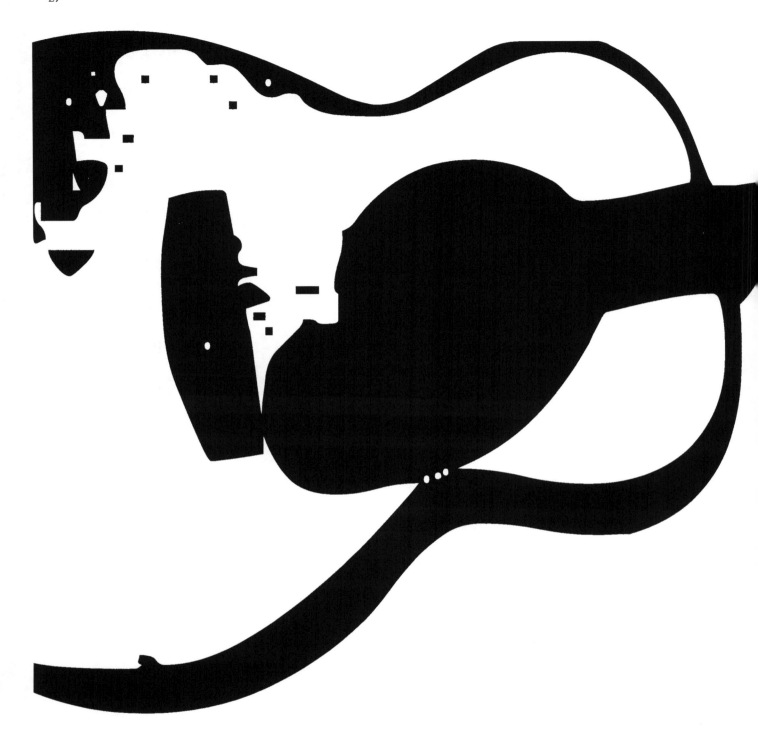

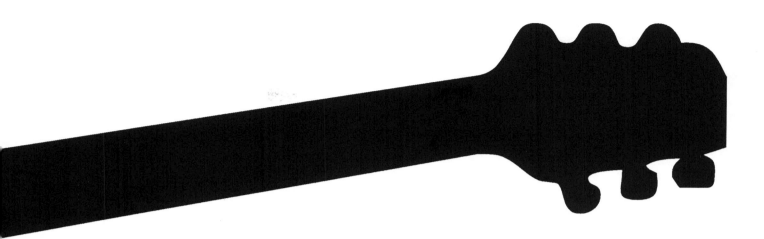

THE D CHORDS AND SCALES

OR
"THE ①ST / ⑥TH STRING(S), 2ND FINGER SHAPES"

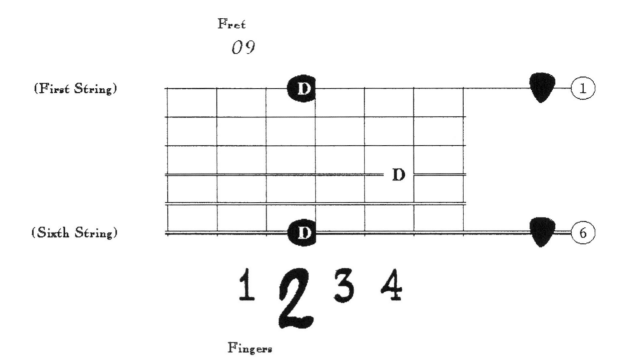

Fret
09

(First String) ... 1

D

D

(Sixth String) ... 6

1 2 3 4

Fingers

THE ABOVE "FIRST / SIXTH STRING(S) SECOND FINGER" SHAPE CONSTRUCT UNDERSCORES ALL NINTH POSITION D CHORDS AND SCALES. THE RATHER IMPORTANT **MAIN** D ROOT NOTE(S) ARE FIXED ON THE FIRST / SIXTH STRING(S), UNDERNEATH THE SECOND FINGER, THAT FINGER FRETTING. THE LARGE **MAIN** D ROOT NOTE(S) "DOT(S)" GROUND THE FINGER WORK INVOLVED. THAT SAID, THE FOURTH STRING D, THE ONLY D LEFT, IS PLACED IN THE MIDDLE OF THE TWO OCTAVES WITH THE PINKY FRETTING. ☞

Some of the D chord voicings associated with the guitar's ninth position are:

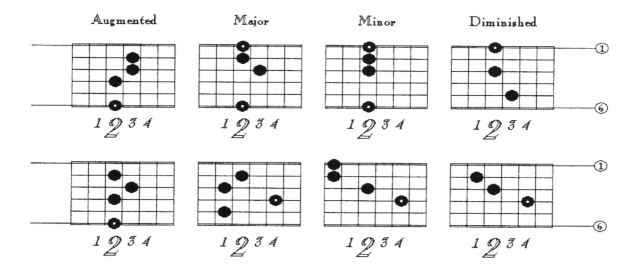

Some of the D scale voicings associated with the guitar's ninth position are:

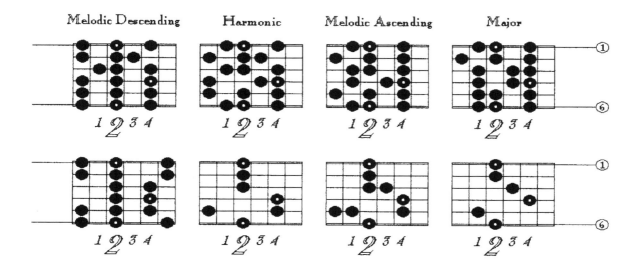

FURTHER COMMENTARY...

ALL D CHORDS AND SCALES SITUATE THEMSELVES IN THE NINTH POSITION FRAMEWORK SO SHREWDLY, AND ALL SUBSEQUENT FORMS AND PATTERNS TAKEN FROM HERE WILL ALSO FIT IN ANY OTHER POSITION TOO. AS NOW EVIDENCED IN THE GRIDS ON THE EARLIER PAGE, THE SECOND AND FOURTH FINGERS COORDINATE BEST WHEN PLAYING THE D MATERIAL; THE D ROOT ON THE FOURTH STRING GETTING INVOLVED IN THE FINGERING OFTEN. ALSO, RECOGNIZE THE "DOT(S)" GROUND THE FINGER WORK, BUT BEYOND THAT, IT'S IMPORTANT TO UNDERSTAND THE SECOND FINGER'S TECHNICAL ROLE AS IT FRETS EITHER **MAIN** D ROOT NOTE(S) ONE AT A TIME, OR BOTH VIA BARRE TECHNIQUE. IT MIGHT FIND ITSELF UNINTENTIONALLY BARRING A STRING OR TWO WHEN DOING SO, THE DOUBLE STOP IN THIS POSITION BEING AN EXCELLENT EXAMPLE OF THIS. THE DOUBLE

STOP HERE NECESSITATES THAT THE SECOND FINGER BARRE ITS TOP TWO THINNEST STRINGS. BUT EVEN WHEN OTHER FINGERS MUST SHARE THE FRET SPACE, THE SECOND FINGER STILL PRESIDES AS EITHER **MAIN** D ROOT NOTE(S) FALL BENEATH IT.

EACH D DISCUSSED HERE MUSICALLY FUNCTIONS ONE IN THE SAME REGARDING ITS TRUE PURPOSE. EITHER D NEED NOT BE VOICED EVERY TIME THOUGH, NOR AT EVERY OCCASION, IN WHICHEVER GIVEN D CHORDS AND SCALES ARE USED.

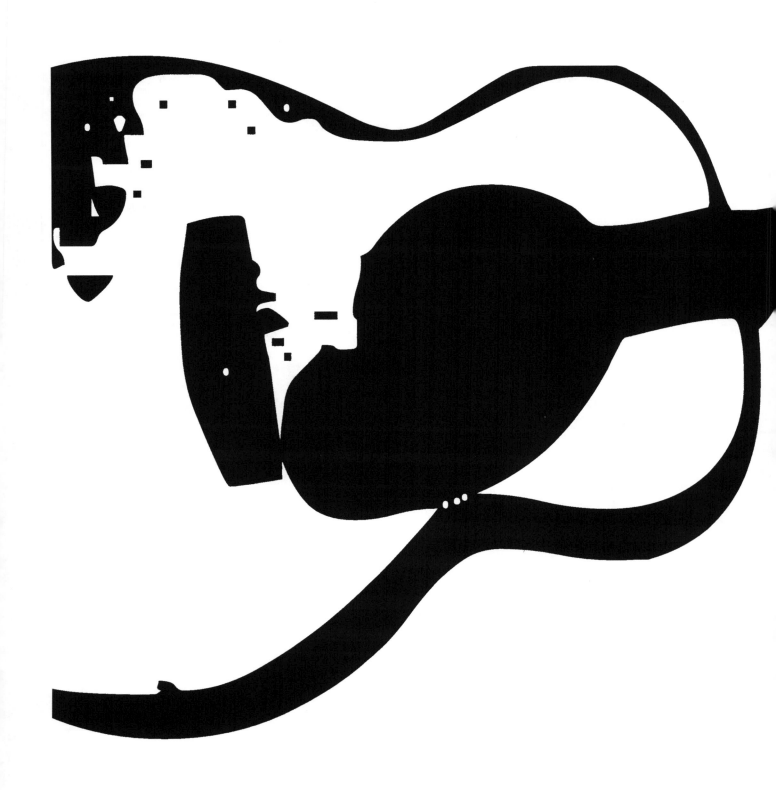

Alphabetical Appendix

Fret
09

(Second String)

1 **2** 3 4

Fingers

THE A CHORDS AND SCALES

OR
"THE ②ND STRING, 2ND FINGER SHAPES"

②ND, 2ND - A CHORDS

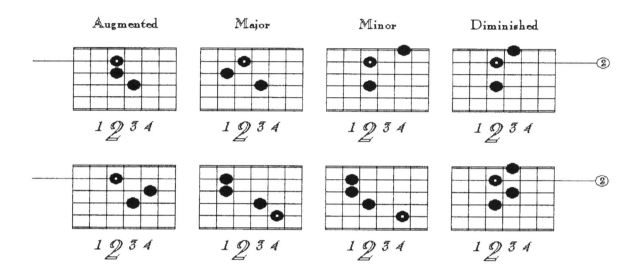

Augmented   Major   Minor   Diminished

②ND, 2ND - A SCALES

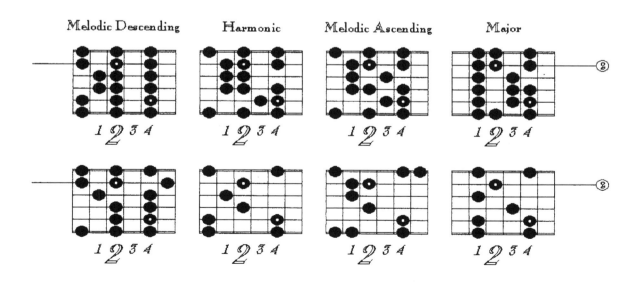

Melodic Descending   Harmonic   Melodic Ascending   Major

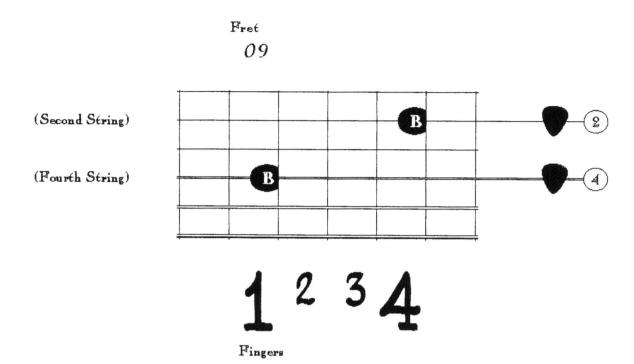

Fret

09

(Second String)

(Fourth String)

1 2 3 4

Fingers

THE B CHORDS AND SCALES

OR
"THE ②ᴺᴰ / ④ᵀᴴ STRING(S), 1ˢᵀ & 4ᵀᴴ FINGER(S) SHAPES"

②ND ④TH, 1ST & 4TH - B CHORDS

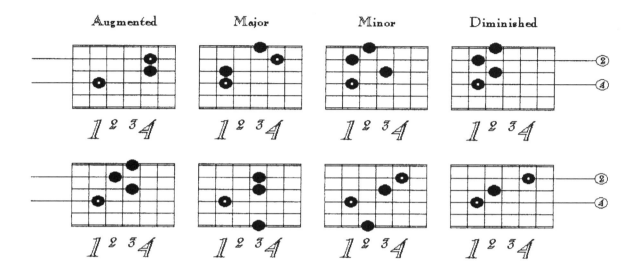

②ND ④TH, 1ST & 4TH - B SCALES

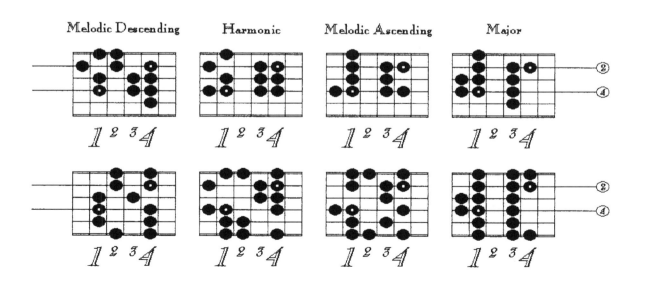

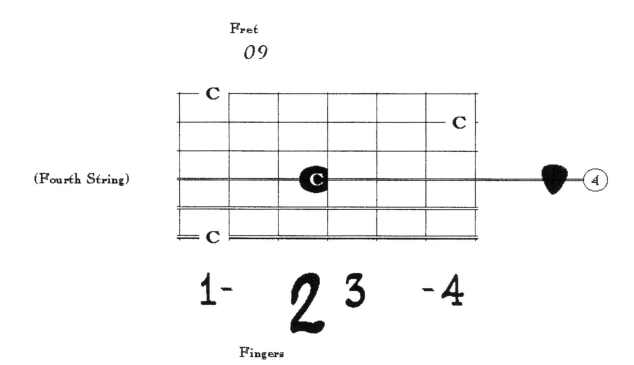

THE C CHORDS AND SCALES

OR

"THE ④TH STRING, 2ND FINGER SHAPES"

④TH, 2ND – C CHORDS

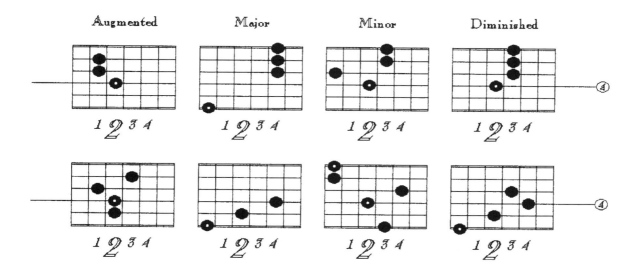

④TH, 2ND – C SCALES

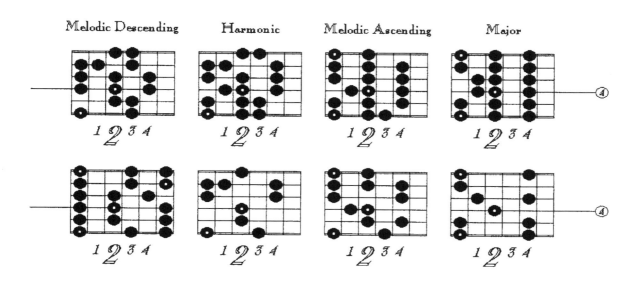

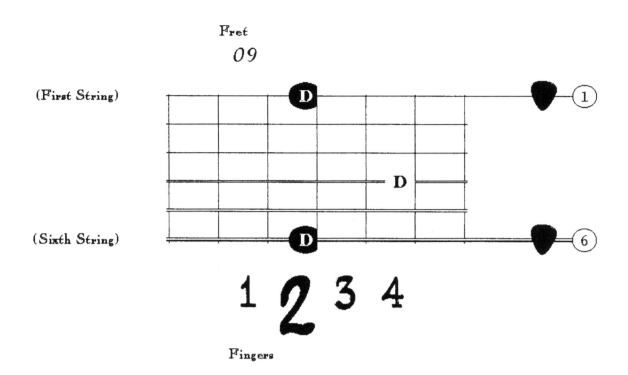

THE D CHORDS AND SCALES

OR

"THE ①ˢᵀ / ⑥ᵀᴴ STRING(S), 2ᴺᴰ FINGER(S) SHAPES"

①ˢᵀ ⑥ᵀᴴ, 2ᴺᴰ –D CHORDS

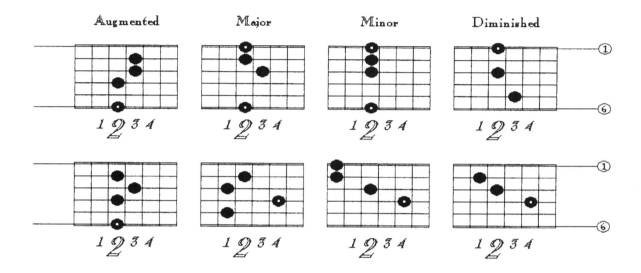

Augmented   Major   Minor   Diminished

①ˢᵀ ⑥ᵀᴴ, 2ᴺᴰ –D SCALES

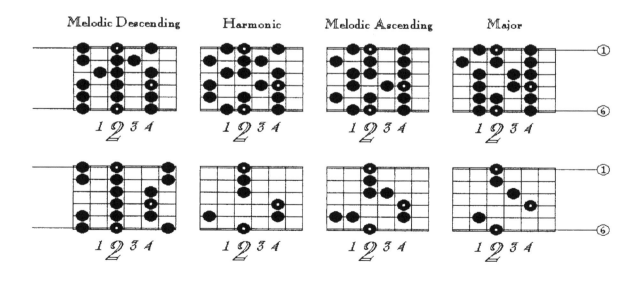

Melodic Descending   Harmonic   Melodic Ascending   Major

Fret

09

(First String)

(Third String)

(Sixth String)

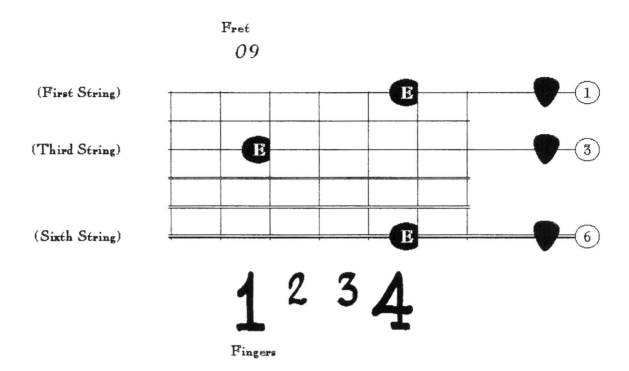

Fingers

THE E CHORDS AND SCALES

OR

"THE ①ST / ③RD / ⑥TH STRING(S), 1ST & 4TH FINGER(S) SHAPES"

①ˢᵗ ③ʳᵈ ⑥ᵗʰ, 1ˢᵗ & 4ᵗʰ –E Chords

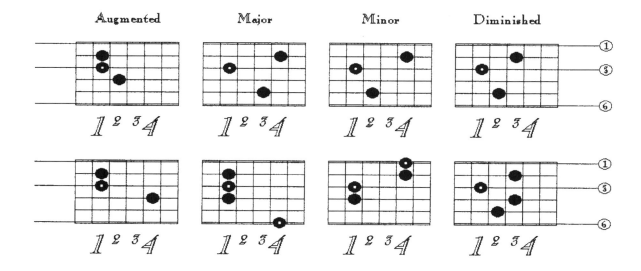

①ˢᵗ ③ʳᵈ ⑥ᵗʰ, 1ˢᵗ & 4ᵗʰ –E Scales

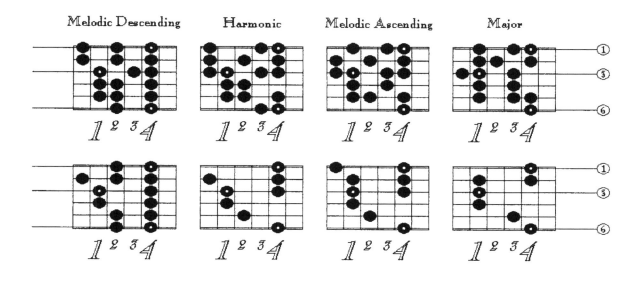

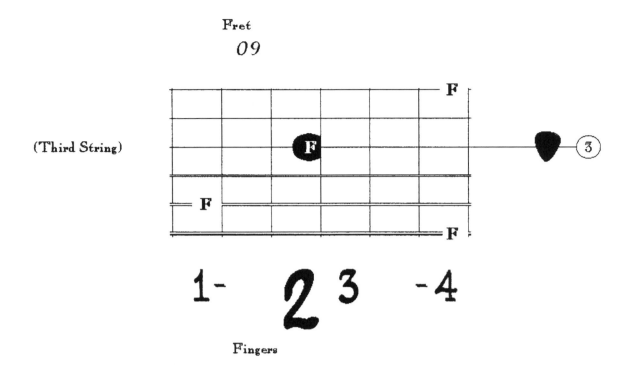

Fret
09

(Third String)

Fingers

THE **F** CHORDS AND SCALES

OR
"THE ③ʳᵈ STRING, 2ⁿᵈ FINGER SHAPES"

③RD, 2ND -F CHORDS

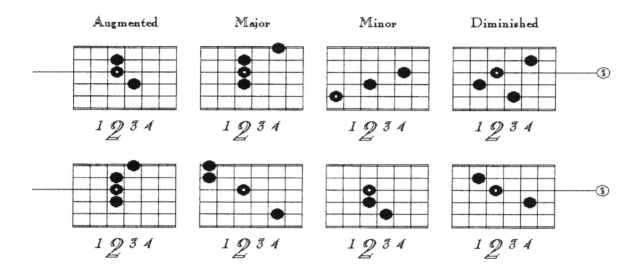

Augmented   Major   Minor   Diminished

1 2 3 4   1 2 3 4   1 2 3 4   1 2 3 4

1 2 3 4   1 2 3 4   1 2 3 4   1 2 3 4

③RD, 2ND -F SCALES

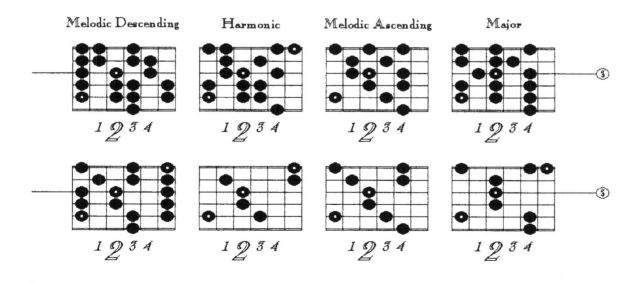

Melodic Descending   Harmonic   Melodic Ascending   Major

1 2 3 4   1 2 3 4   1 2 3 4   1 2 3 4

1 2 3 4   1 2 3 4   1 2 3 4   1 2 3 4

Fret
09

(Fifth String)

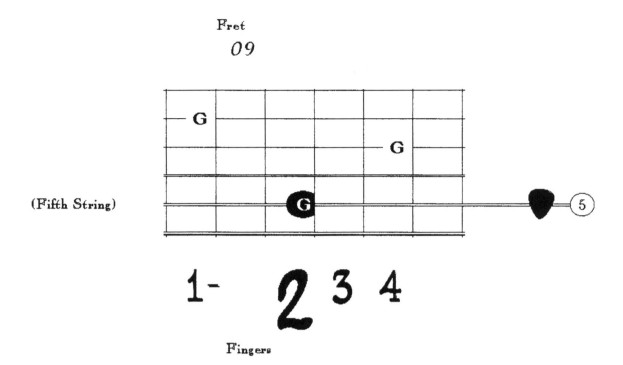

Fingers

THE G CHORDS AND SCALES

OR
"THE ⑤TH STRING, 2ND FINGER SHAPES"

⑤TH, 2ND – G CHORDS

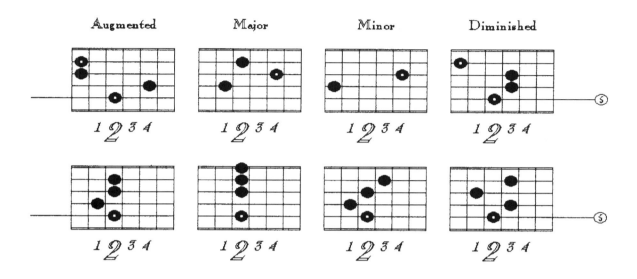

⑤TH, 2ND – G SCALES

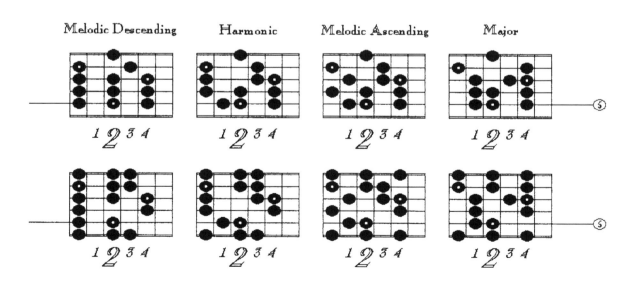

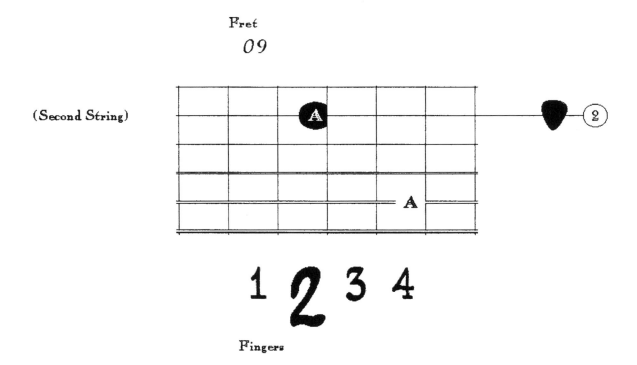

The A Chords and Scales

or
"The ②ND String, 2ND Finger Shapes"

②ND, 2ND -A CHORDS

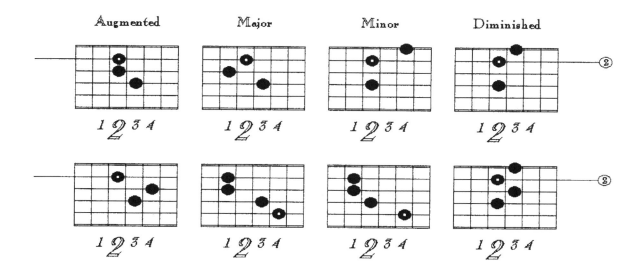

Augmented · Major · Minor · Diminished

②ND, 2ND -A SCALES

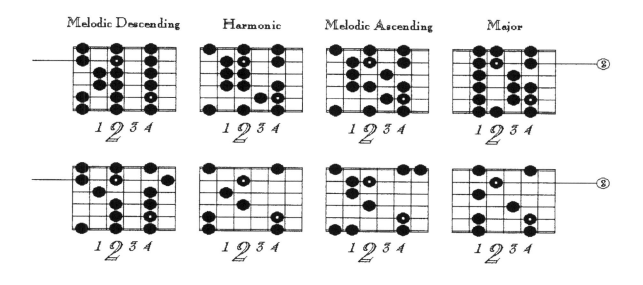

Melodic Descending · Harmonic · Melodic Ascending · Major

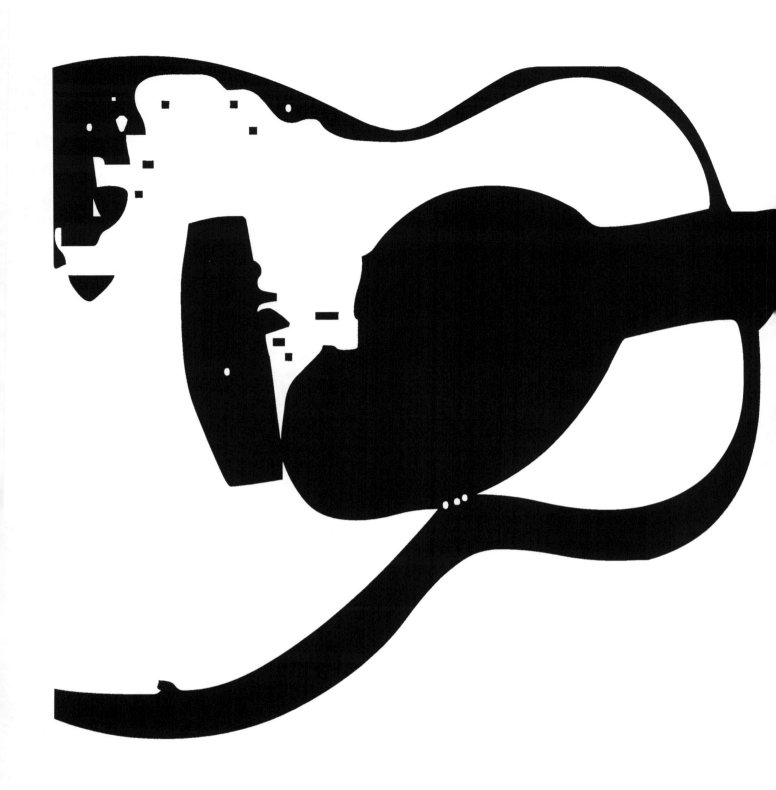

Notation & Tablature

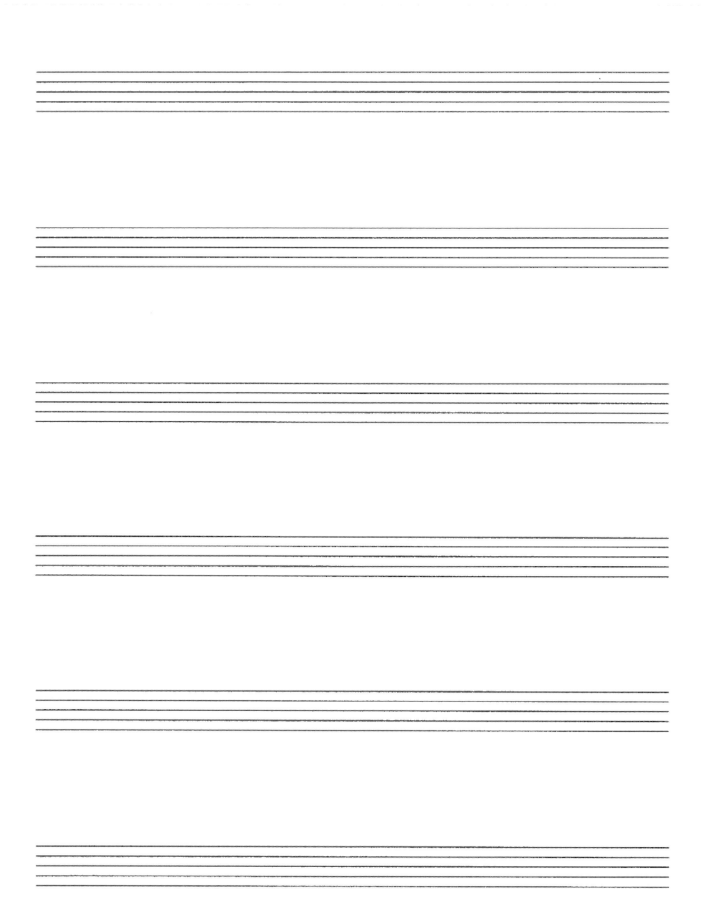

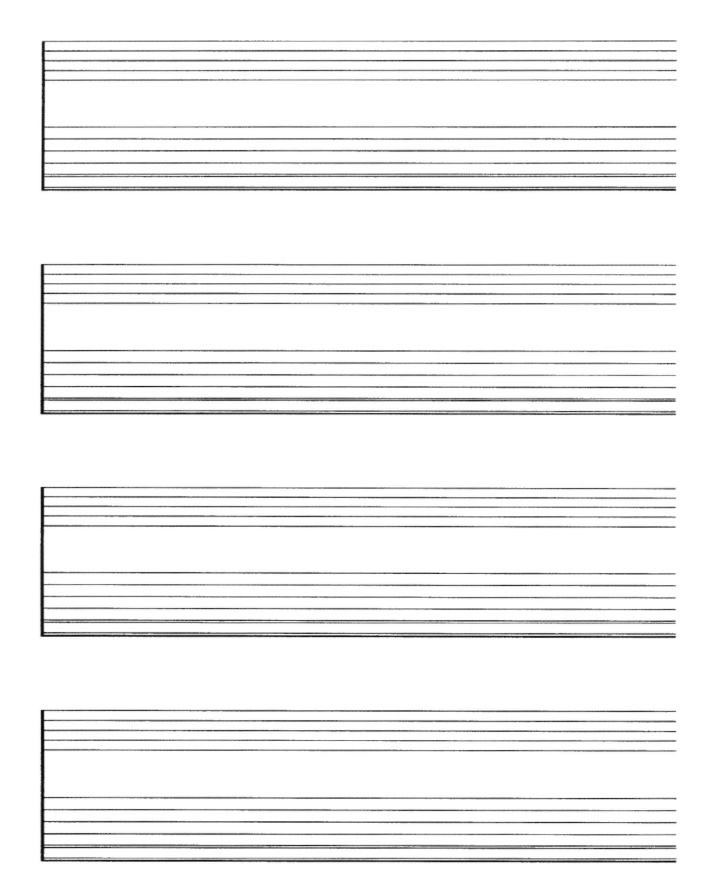

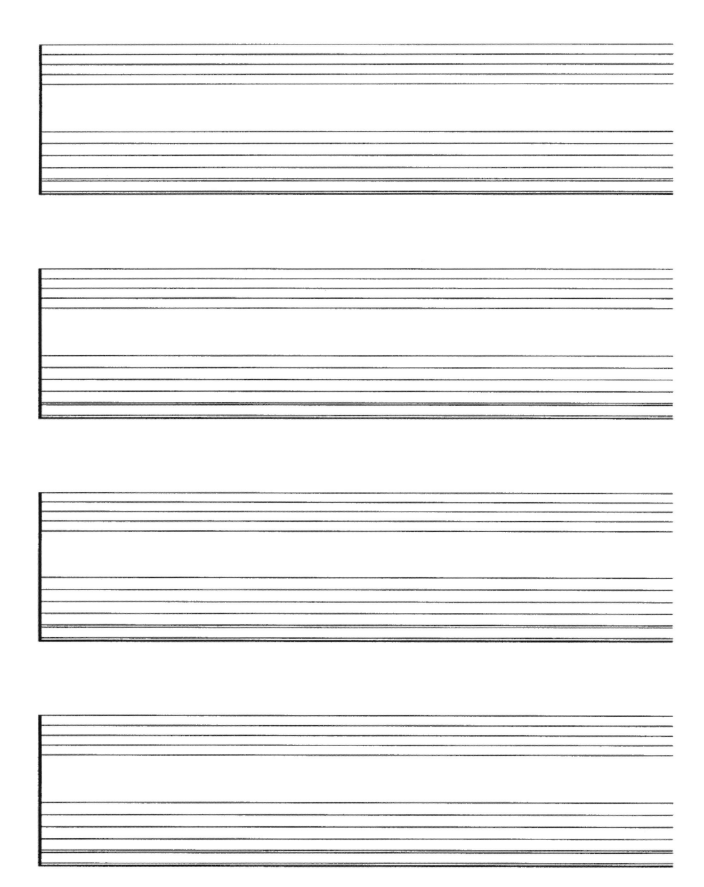

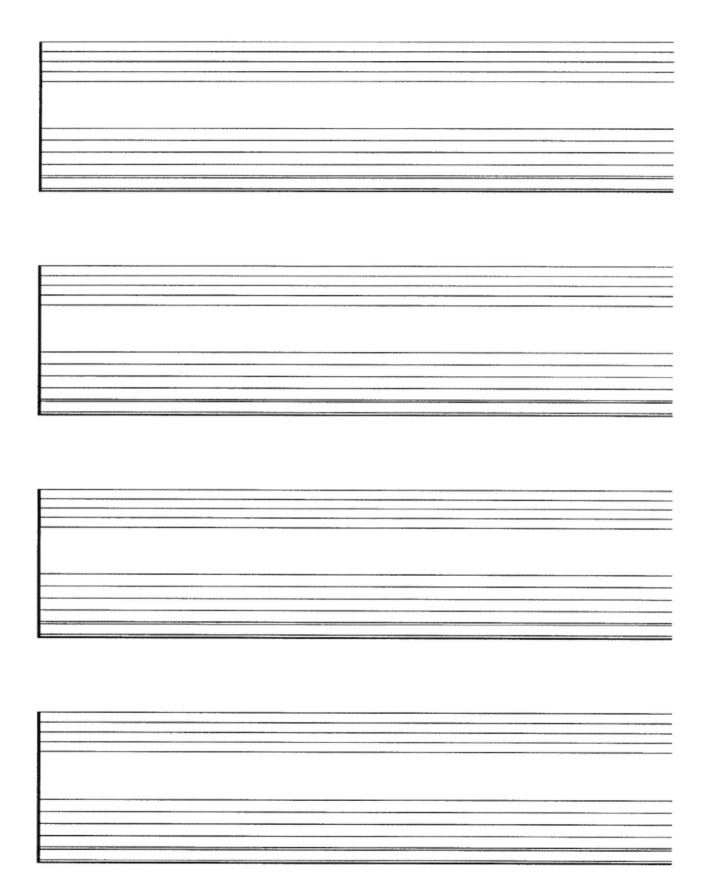

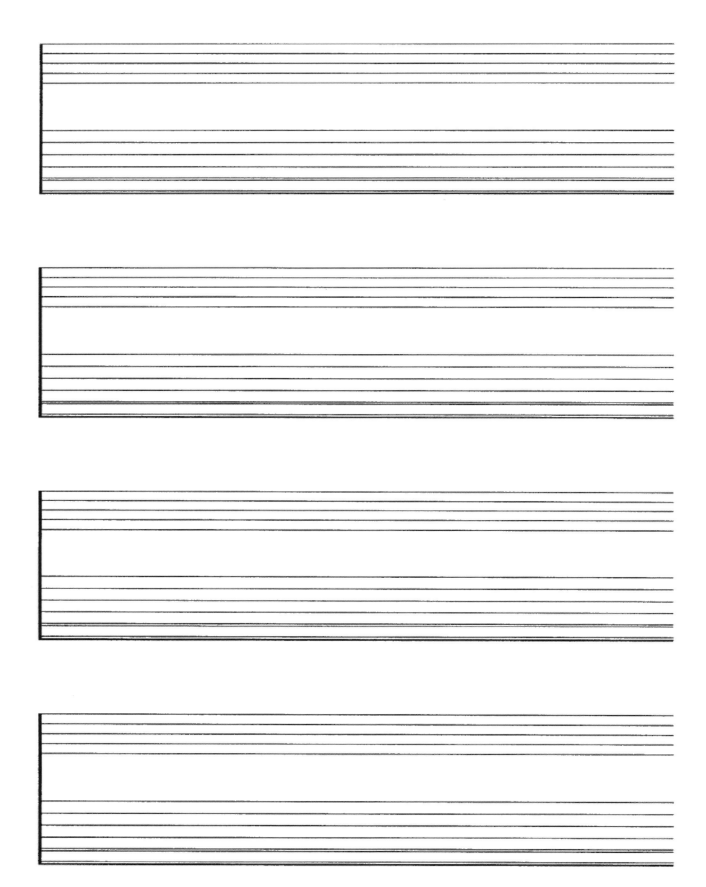

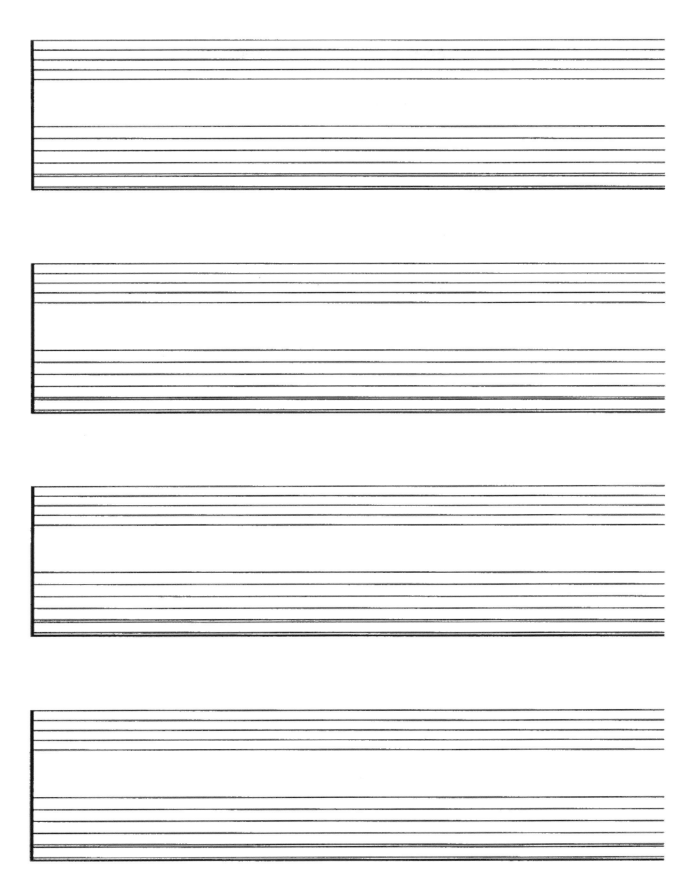

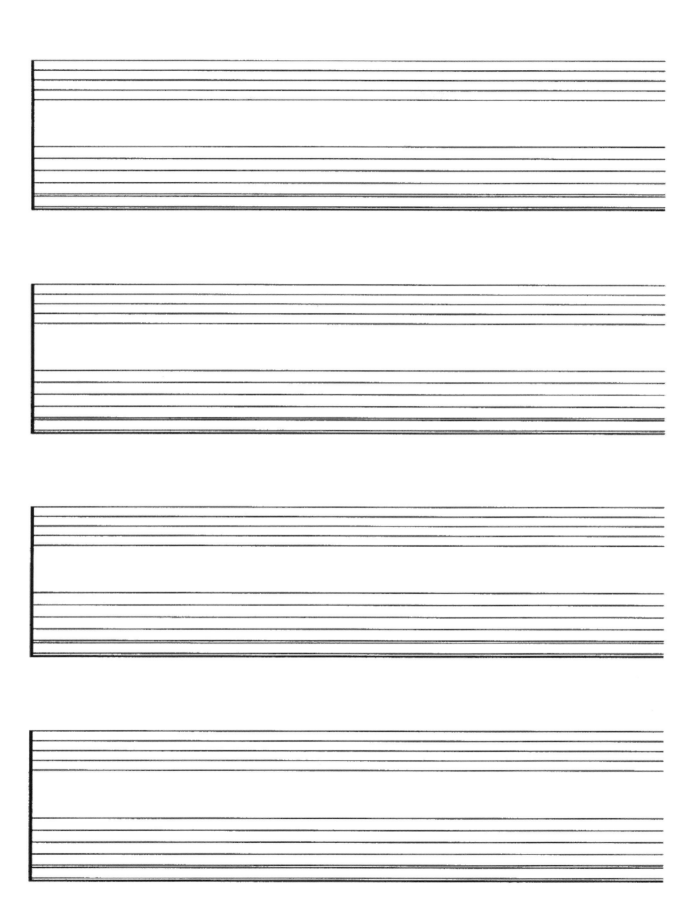

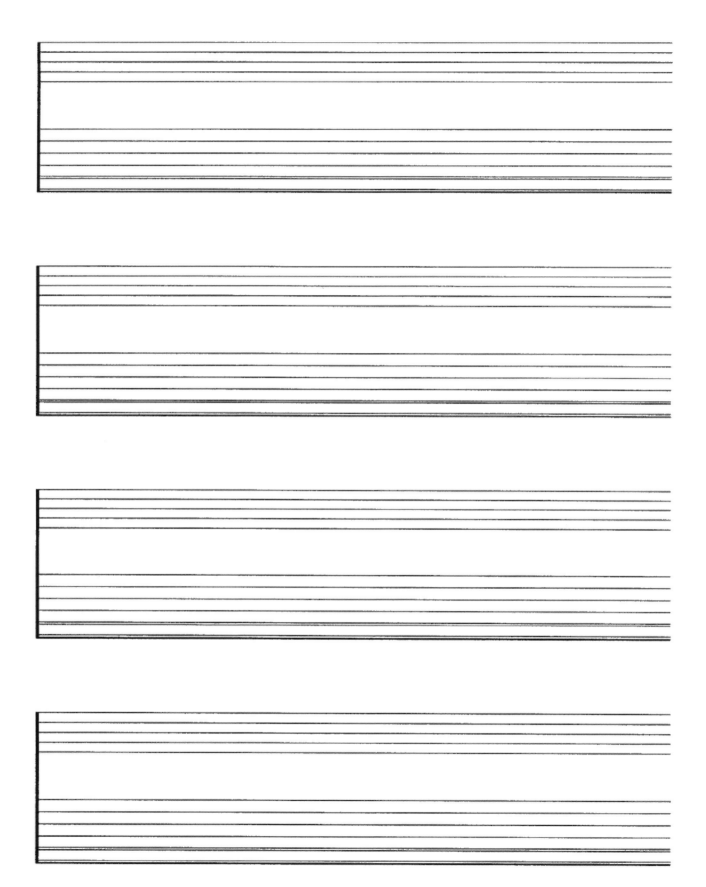

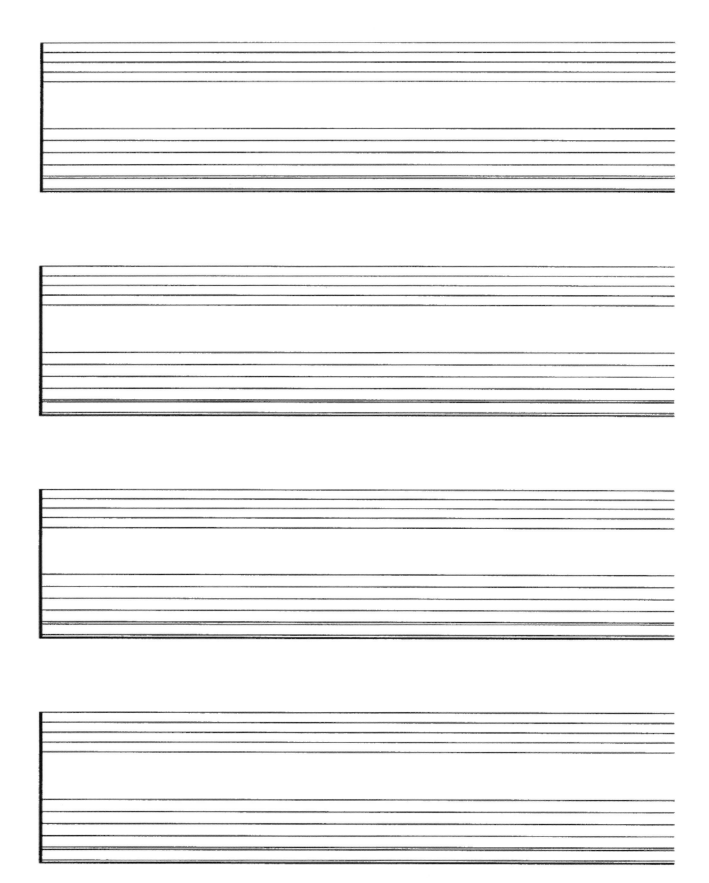

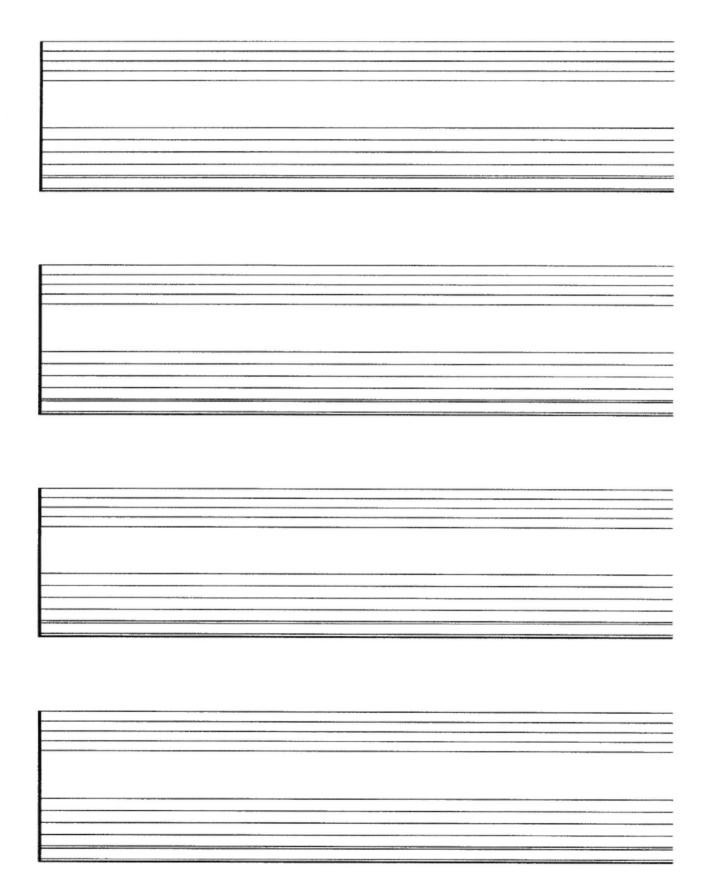

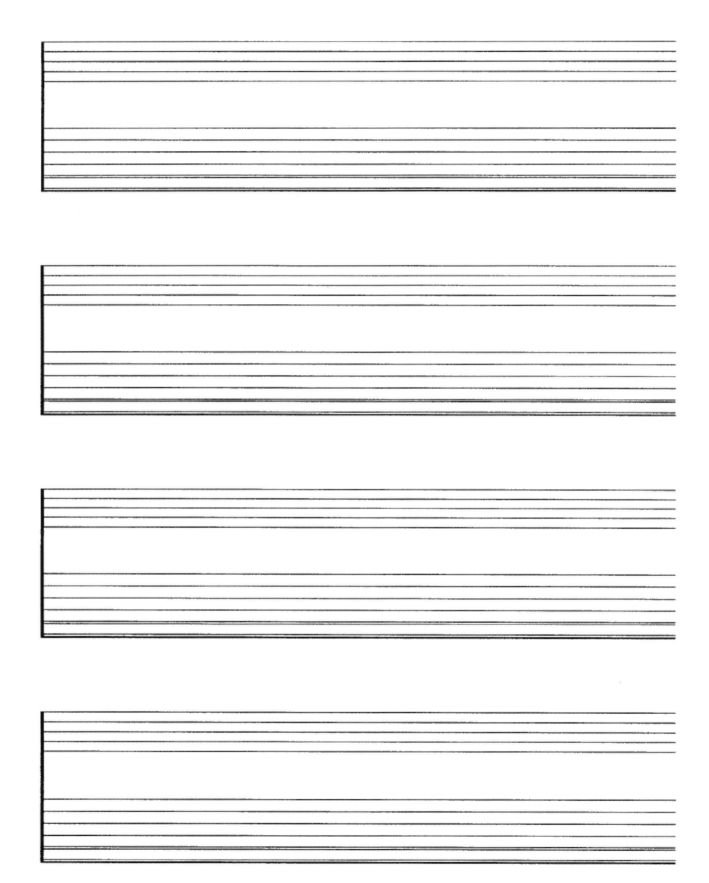

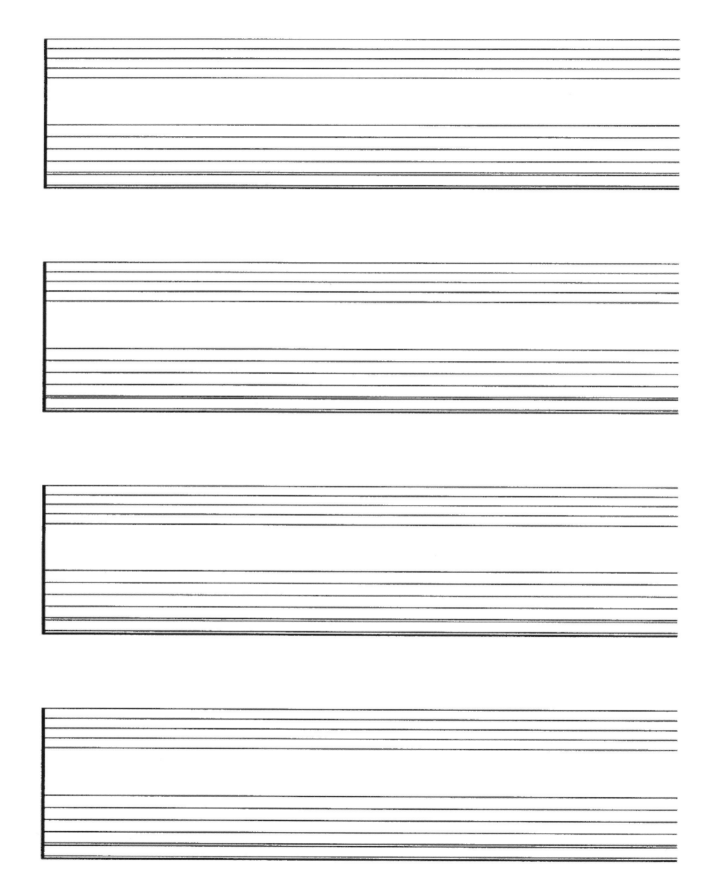

Made in United States
Troutdale, OR
02/23/2024